Intuition

THE JOURNAL OF A MASTER PSYCHIC

MICHAEL DEAN

Printed in the United States of America

ISBN 978-1-4303-1681-7

This book is dedicated to my sons, Michael, Dustin, and Tyson. Thank you for all of the love and laughter you have given me. I sincerely love you all three with all of my heart. It is my greatest joy to be your father.

To my wife Lisa, thank you for teaching me how to open my heart and to love.

To Sonia Choquette, thank you for teaching me to believe in myself and my inner creator.

May God bless you all!

Contents

Part I: Psychic Journey

Part II: Common Psychic Channels & Tools to Sharpen them

Part III:

Testimonies

"The guidance that I have received from Michael has been life changing for me. His compassion combined with accuracy and his intuitiveness has given me great confidence in his readings. As a healer, Michael has the ability to reach into your soul and touch it. You can feel his healing powers." Donna Jackson

"Michael has the ability to advise people along their journey of life with accuracy and compassion. He truly is an inspiration. He has a gift that is meant to be shared with others and I consider myself privileged that our paths have crossed." Dana Fearn

Every story in this book is true, most of the names have been changed to protect the privacy of those involved.

Chapter 1

MY TRIP TO CASSADAGA FLORIDA

Cassadaga is a spiritualist camp located about a half hour away from Daytona Beach Florida. While on vacation with my wife and sons, we decided to go to Cassadaga to get readings. Something I have always wanted to do in Florida and a place I always wanted to visit.

Cassadaga is a beautiful historic town, around 100 years old. As we pulled in, I got this sort of nostalgic feeling. It is a very comfortable place to be and the people there are a delight to be around.

I had a reading by a very nice lady, who for her privacy's sake, we will call her Helen. Helen was a very humbled lady, in her early forty's, I would guess. She used a technique called psychometry, this is where you hold an object that belongs to someone and are able to read the vibrations from the person in the object.

During my reading Helen told me that I was very intuitive and that she saw me doing readings as well. She said, "I see you going to Chicago to further your psychic training. I also see you in Indianapolis." She also told me she saw me writing and teaching as well.

After the reading I went to the bookstore at Cassadaga and picked up a couple of stones that caught my eye, and a few books. I really didn't have time to check the books out that well, I really just looked at the covers, picked them out and went on. My sons were saying they were hungry and wanted to eat at the Cassadaga restaurant. So, I hurried with my book selections. After we ate and spent a few nights in Orlando, we decided to return back home to Indiana.

Once we settled back in, I started reading on the first book. It was the Psychic Pathway by Sonia Choquette. It was a very interesting and informative book. It helped a great deal on raising my vibration and awareness. As I was finishing the book, I noticed it said for more information, contact Sonia Choquette, Chicago, Illinois.

I decided to call, and I spoke to Sonia's assistant. I asked him about Sonia's training classes. We discussed that for a few minutes. I said, "you know I would love to meet Sonia, she sounds very interesting and intelligent." He then asked me where I lived and wanted to know how far was I from Indianapolis. I told him I lived about and hour and a half from there.

He said, "guess what?" Sonia is going to be in Indianapolis this weekend. I was so excited about it, I couldn't wait to go. Her assistant told me, "everything happens for a reason, it looks like you got this one in perfect timing."

I waited anxiously for Saturday to come. Finally, it was here and I went to Indianapolis to Sonia's class. When I meet Sonia, she was everything I expected her to be. She was wonderful and very intelligent, so intuitive, and she was such a pleasure to meet.

I spoke with Sonia and got information on her psychic training classes. I found out that I could take some of them online. Which would work very well with me.

After I got home, I registered for Sonia's online classes, and began taking them. After completing the online course, there was a class being held in Chicago, that I registered for.

I attended Sonia's psychic certification training class, and I am now on my psychic pathway.

Chapter 2

MY SPIRIT GUIDE CHUCK

One night last summer, I was up late playing on the computer. It was around 3:30 in the morning. There was no-one else up. As I sat there playing on my computer, I guess I kind of went into a trance, without really knowing it.

My friend, who we will call Chuck, had passed away about six months before, came to me as plain as day and said, "Mike, Earl is here with us." Earl was also a close friend of mine and Chucks'. I also worked with Earl for about eight years. The last time I had spoken with Earl, he seemed to be fine.

After I saw Chuck, I went into my bedroom and woke my wife, Lisa up and told her what had just happened. I then wrote it in my journal and went on to bed.

Late the next evening, I went to get gas in my car and I ran into a guy that I use to work with. We talked about the local police department where I used to work. My friend, Bill, then quickly changed the subject, and asked me if I heard about Earl. I told him that I hadn't heard anything. He told me that Earl had passed away during the night and that the hospital staff had put him on a respirator until all of the family could get there. I didn't know what to say, I was in shock. Four days later I had attended Earls funeral.

That night Chuck came to me was so vividly clear. I know

why he did, because I wasn't trying to. Sometimes when you try, you try too hard. So, on my six sensory journey, this has taught me a very valuable lesson. Not to try so hard, because when you do, your not allowing spirits to come through as they want to. Rather your trying to get them to come to you, your way and it simply doesn't work. So, just sit back, relax and let it flow.

Chapter 3

A GIFT FROM MY SPIRIT GUIDE

One night I was reading a book by my teacher Sonia Choquette. In the book she writes about asking your spirit guides to surprise you with a gift and they will.

As I laid down and said my nightly prayers, I talked to my spirit guide Chuck. I asked him to surprise me with a gift. After talking to Chuck, I laid in my bed wondering what Chuck would surprise me with and how long it would take.

I slowly drifted off to sleep. The next morning I got up and got ready for work as usual. When I arrived at work at my Tanning Salon, I went in and turned the open sign on, no sooner than I done that, my friend Toby came in carrying a beautiful house plant. Toby said, "Good morning," sitting the beautiful peace lily on the counter.

Toby said, "I got up this morning and was sitting at my kitchen table, drinking coffee looking at this plant and out of the blue something told me that Chuck would want you to have it." He said he had about 3 or 4 more at his house. All of them came from Chucks funeral. He also told me, that he knew Chuck and I were very good friend, and he thought he would bring it to me.

I then told Toby about me asking Chuck to surprise me with a gift. Toby said, "wow, that is really something else. Now I know he wanted me to bring this to you."

We talked for a while reminiscing about the past. That was normally what we did when ever we would see each other, which is not that often.

Toby then left and I was still excited about the peace lily and how quickly Chuck had come through for me.

Sonia was right on as well. So, my advise would be, don't be shy, speak up and ask your guides to surprise you with a gift, and they will. It is a very heart felt moment when your guides show you they care by responding to your call.

Chapter 4

DISBELIEVING EARS

My wife Lisa was pregnant with our third son, Tyson and was in her last 3 weeks of pregnancy. She had a doctors appointment for that following Friday for a weekly check-up. Everything had been going very well for her.

It was on a Wednesday, and my vibes told me that the doctor would want to put her in the hospital on the day of her check-up. I told Lisa what my vibes had told me that they would want to admit her on Friday, so I told her to be prepared. But of course she was already packed and ready to go, and after I told her what my vibes told me, she finished getting all the last minute things together. She knew she needed to be prepared, because I was almost right on everything, because over the years she has witnessed several of my psychic abilities.

Friday morning came, and I told Lisa, to call me at work and let me know what all the doctor tells her. I kissed her and our older two boys bye and headed out the door to go to work.

Later on that day while I was at work, the phone rings, it

was Lisa. She told me that the doctor was sending her to the hospital and wanted to admit her because her blood pressure was very high and they want to keep an eye on her and the baby.

Even though it was the third time Lisa had given birth, she sounded pretty scared and nervous and she even started to cry. I told her that everything is going to be okay and I told her that I would leave work and head on up to the hospital. Lisa's mom was at our house with Dustin and was going to be there to keep Michael when he got home from school.

When I arrived at the hospital the doctor was in the room talking to Lisa. He told me that she was dilated to two centimeters and that her blood pressure was high and they wanted to keep an eye on her and Tyson.

After the doctor left the room, I told Lisa not to worry that Tyson would not be born until on the 9th of October, which was on Sunday, two days away. Our other two boys were also born on the 9th but in different months.

The next morning, which was Saturday, the doctor came in and said that everything looks good and they would go ahead and let Lisa go home. They told her to get plenty of rest and take it easy because she only had three weeks to go.

I then looked at the doctor and laughed and told him that my guides told me that Tyson was going to be born tomorrow. The doctor looked at me and asked, "you believe in that stuff?"

I said, "yes."

He then asked me if I thought I was a psychic or something and I told him that I was, he just said okay, like he thought I was crazy, and smirked in disbelief.

Lisa and I head home. We had ordered pizza that night and our friend Nathan was at the house. Lisa was standing in front of the stove, and I went over to her and put my arms around her and rubbed her on the stomach and said, "he will be here tomorrow."

She looked at me with a huge smile on her face and said, "I have always believed in you, and I have seen a lot, but if he is really does come tomorrow, I know you are for real."

After we finished eating, we put the baby bed together and Lisa cleaned his room spotless, and finished washing all of his clothes. She stayed up until four in the morning and then we went to bed.

My guides were right on, because at 6:30 a.m. that morning, Lisa's water broke. We had only gotten 2 ½ hours of sleep. And you guessed it, it was Sunday morning, October the 9th.

I called Lisa's mom and she came and got the boys and they were going to get ready to come to the hospital.

We arrived at the hospital, and before the doctor had come in, I got this heavy feeling in my stomach. I didn't tell Lisa, because I didn't want her to get scared or upset. I called on my healer guides and I called on sitting bull, then I just relaxed, knowing whatever the feeling was that my request to my healer guide's would be heard.

The lady that was going to give Lisa an epidural came in, she was an Indian woman, who looked like she was in her late forty's. The doctor then came in to check Lisa and said well, we need to go ahead and move you into the delivery room.

Just then, Lisa's mom, Michael and Dustin, her brothers Elijah, Harrison, Charlie, Brian and his family, and my sister

Billie arrived. They all got to speak with Lisa for a few minutes. The nurse came in and said she was going to get the doctor back in and they would have her to start pushing.

Everyone kissed Lisa bye, and told her they would be right out in the waiting room.

Our oldest son, Michael stayed in the delivery room with us, to watch his baby brother be born. As Tyson started crowning and started to come out, the nurse said, "cord times two." The umbilical cord was wrapped around Tyson's neck twice. The nurse took over and delivered Tyson, getting that cord removed from around his neck and then Tyson was born and he was okay and very healthy.

I know that the credit goes to my healer guide sitting bull, because the situation was taken care of so swiftly by the nurse. I know sitting bull had sent her to us that day.

After the delivery, that doctor asked, "what time is it?"

The nurse told him what time it was and what day it was. Before the doctor even wrote it down, he turned and looked at me like he had just seen a ghost. I just looked at him with a big grin and said, "I told you we would be back and that he would be born today."

He turned to Lisa and said, "does this kind of stuff happen a lot with you guys?"

Lisa smiled and said, "yes, and our other two boys were also born on the 9th, Michael was born on January the 9th and Dustin was born on March the 9th."

The doctor said, "that is so freaky." He asked the nurse, "what were the chances of that?"

Needless to say, when the doctor left the room he didn't have that "Mr. know it all smirk" on his face, and as for the nurse, well I truly believe that she was God sent.

Part II

Common Psychic Channels
And Tools to sharpen them

Chapter 5

COMMON PSYCHIC CHANNELS

CLAIRAUDIENCE

Clairaudience, means clear hearing. Location, crown chakra. At first it may come in thought forms. Because you cannot hear It psychically doesn't mean that you are not clairaudience. If you are talking to someone and thoughts pop into your mind that seems to come from nowhere, that is clairaudience.

To sharpen this ability, meditation in a very quite room will work, no music, nothing but silence. After you have cleared your mind, start asking yourself questions, you will be very surprised to find that you do in fact hear the voice aloud, just like another person was right next to you talking.

It may sound like your voice or a voice that you are familiar with, or even an unknown voice. If you think back, this has already happened to you before. Just as you begin to fall asleep, when you start dreaming, you can hear voices in the dream. Right? Well, that is the same thing, only thing is you are awake. So, find a quite place where you know you wont be bothered and let the voices begin.

CLAIRVOYANCE

Clairvoyance means clear seeing or psychic seeing. This energy source is located between your eyes about one half to one inch above the nose. Clairvoyance is the ability to see people, places, and objects in your minds eye.

Your imagination is the key to sharpening this ability. Close your eyes and relax. Once you are relaxed, start trying to visualize images in your mind. I close my eyes and I visualize a hose up against my third eye, and then I imagine what I might see at the other end of the hose.

You will want to visualize every detail that you can, and focus only on that object. This is also called remote viewing. As well, when practicing, you should always keep a positive mind set. Do not focus on negative things. I would recommend not doing it on a day that has been stressful.

Once your third eye gets better developed, have someone place an object in a box, but not tell you what it is. Then go in another room and try to view the object in detail.

Remember, if you don't view it accurate the first time, don't give up, you will need a lot of practice to develop this technique.

CLAIRSENTIENCE

Clairsentience means sensing; the ability to sense things clearly. When you are around people, places or objects, and the hair on your arms and the back of your neck stand up, cold chills, gut feelings, nervousness, and your heart pounds, pay special attention to these signs, because your body is trying to tell you something.

To sharpen this ability, when you are around people, places, objects, or situations, ask yourself, how does this person or place make me feel. Does it make me fee comfortable, or does it drain me?

Pay close attention to your vibes, and these feelings. If you don't like the way you feel, or you are not comfortable around certain people or places, you need to leave.

Our bodies absorb these energies from other people and places. Don't let your body absorb these energies that drain you. Make you fearful or isn't supportive of a positive nature.

Clairsentience psychometry is another technique that is helpful in sharpening your ability. Psychometry is holding or touching objects and reading the vibes from them.

Chapter 6

PRECOGNITION

Precognition is the ability to perceive information about the future, places or events before they occur. This one is pretty common with most people for example you and one of your friends are talking about a song that neither one of you have heard for a quite sometime, only to find that when you turn the radio on, the song is just starting to play. You both were receiving information from each other and the universe. You were just not consciously aware of it until after the fact, when you heard the song and it gets your attention. In essence you had become a form of trance state at oneness with the universe. Then you snap out of it when you heard the song.

One of my favorite stories of precognition happened to me in 1988. I was a teenager working part-time in a restaurant. My shift had ended and it was time for me to wait for my ride to pick me up. While I was sitting there at a booth waiting on him to show up, a fellow co-worker, that was waiting to clock in, sat down with to until time to do so.

As we sat there waiting, making conversation over our milk shakes, my co-worker asked me what kind of car was my ride going to be picking me up in, so he could help me watch for him.

I started joking with him about Pete, the guy who was picking me up, because Pete had an old beat up truck. I mean, a real lush, a lemon. I told my co-worker, jokingly, that Pete was going to be picking me up in a brand new Lincoln, it was gray with leather seats. I also told him that the car was loaded.

A few more minutes had passed, then my co-worker said, "hey your ride just pulled up." I said, "where?"

He said, "right there," pointing to a beautiful Lincoln.

The man sitting in the Lincoln was Pete. I was in complete disbelief! I had made up the whole story of the car, because I wanted to see him laugh when he saw Pete's old beat up truck pull up.

Looking back now, I not only knew subconsciously, that he had bought a new car, what color it was, that it was a Lincoln, and that it had all leather seats. Not to mention, my Co-worker knew what to look for, because he was the one that spotted him.

So, see there was a reason for me to make up that story, I just didn't consciously know it. To sharpen your precognition abilities, pay attention to your thoughts as well, you may even want to make notes of them.

PRECOGNITON PART 2

In 2004, I had been thinking of my friend Pete a lot. I hadn't spoken to him or seen him for about 15 years. I told my wife, Lisa about it. She said, "well, knowing you, you will probably run into him or something like that."

Later that evening, Lisa and I went to our local supermarket. As we were leaving, I saw a man that looked just like Pete. In fact, I actually thought it was him. I went over and spoke to him. I said, "hi Pete."

He told me that his name was not Pete. I told him that he must be his twin or something because he looked just like this man that I know and his name is Pete.

He started laughing and told me that he knew the Pete that I was talking about and that people are all the time thinking that he is Pete. I then started laughing too, I told him that I was sorry that I felt like an idiot.

The man said that Pete lived about 7 miles up the road. I told the man that the last time that I had seen Pete, was in Georgia about 15 years ago. The man said that Pete just moved back to Indiana about a year ago.

I turned and shook the mans hand and told him that it was nice to meet him and that I was sorry for the trouble. He smiled and told me that it was no problem.

Lisa and I left and went on home. On the way home, I told her what had happened while she was in the line checking out. Lisa, looked at me and said, "I bet that is why you have been thinking about Pete lately." That guy looked just like Pete, so I agreed and just left it at that, because I figured she was right.

The very next morning, I got woke up by the phone ringing. I answered, still half asleep, I said, "hello." The voice on the other end said, "are you up yet fat ass?"

I thought, who in the world is this. I asked the man, "who is this?" He said, "it's your dad, you better get up or you are going to be late for school." Then I said, "no, really, who is this, because I don't go to school." I thought maybe it was someone playing a trick on me or something.

The man said, "oh, I am sorry, I must have the wrong number."

I started laughing, the voice sounded so familiar, so I asked again who the guy was. He then told me that his name was Pete. I asked him his last name and he told me what it was. It was the same Pete that I had been thinking about. I told him who I was and he told me that he couldn't believe it. He told me that he had been thinking about me off and on for a few days now.

We sat and talked on the phone for at least a good hour, catching up on everything. It felt so good to reminisce about the past.

It was so incredible, neither one of us had the others phone number, yet we still got connected. It was all because he dialed the wrong number, or did he?

Chapter 7

SING A JOYFULL NOISE UNTO THE LORD

When I was around twenty years old, I worked with a local pest control company. I did inside service as well as outside. This one day, I had an appointment to spray a house in a little town called Crothersville.

On my way to spray the house, I kept hearing a voice tell me, "sing a joyful noise unto the Lord." This happened about three or four times. I thought to myself, "God wants me to sing, so I was singing along with the radio.

As I arrived at the house, a little old lady walked out onto the front porch. She asked me how I was doing. I told her that I was doing fine. She then told me that it was a beautiful day out side today. I looked at her and smiled, and agreed. It was a beautiful day out. The sun was shinning, it was warm out and not too hot. The wind was barley blowing.

I got my equipment ready and went inside to spray. When I got inside, we stood and talked for a few minutes. She was a very pleasant woman to be around. She offered me some lemonade and I accepted.

As I was spraying her house, she asked me if I could spray down in her basement for her. I told her that it would not be a problem, and that I would be more than happy to do it.

After I finished upstairs I went on down into the basement to spray. While I was spraying the basement, there was a huge board leaning against the wall, so I moved it out to get behind it. I looked at the back side of it and noticed it had something written on it with paint. It read, "sing a joyful noise unto the Lord."

I thought, "WOW." This was so amazing. After I finished spraying the basement, I went back up and had the little woman to sign her service ticked. As she was signing the ticket, I told her that I had something strange happen to me today.

I told her about the voice that I had heard on my way to her house, and then about seeing that huge sign in her basement. She told me that she use to be the church choir teacher and that she started getting old so she gave it up, and that she really didn't want to.

We stood and talked for a while and I packed up my stuff and I left. All the way back to the shop, I was thinking that it was so cool, what had happened to me today.

Remember to listen to your inner voice, it knows where you are going before you do.

Chapter 8

MEDITATION

I always begin my meditation sessions by lighting a white candle and burning an incense. Lavender is a great incense to use, because it helps to raise your vibration. You can either lay down or sit in the floor Indian style, you can also sit in a chair. The main things to remember is to make yourself comfortable.

I usually sit in a chair, with my hands on my lap, then I start to clear my mind. It doesn't take long to clear your mind, but if you do have trouble doing so, mentally tell yourself to think about what is on your mind at the time, that you will think about it later. The thoughts will then go away. I found it works best to do it that way.

Have you ever heard someone say, don't think about pink elephants? Well guess what? You think about a pink elephant right off, because you mentally tell yourself not to. So, whatever thoughts you are having, interfering with meditation, try not to think of them, but rather simply say to yourself, I will think about that later and you are giving your conscious mid permission not to think about it. This is mind science, you are pulling the "Jedi mind trick" on your ego allowing you to bypass it .

Once your mind clears, your body also needs to remain

still. After your mind is clear for a few minute, if a thought of a visual image or sound occurs, don't try to edit it or censor it, just
allow it to flow and go with it to see where it takes you.

Meditation is your opportunity for quite and relaxation with great benefits. As you begin to meditate you will begin to hear the voice of your higher self, and your guides.

We weren't designed to run, run, run, we need to shut down mentally, so we can clear our minds and consciousness and when you clear your mind you find you can focus so much better, sleep much better and you won't be as agitated. Remember, meditation is not talking to God, it is listening. We never learn anything by talking, we learn when we clear our minds and listen.

ENTERING A TRANCE STATE

Altered state of consciousness, there are several ways to do this. Drumming works great and so does chanting. Drumming or even listening to beating and chants will help you enter a trance state. Indian drumming CD's work very well for me. I have found that I need a pretty good variety of CD's, because once I have used them a few times, they are not as effective inducing trance.

Having your own drums work very well, because you can mix up the beat to suit your needs, while using your hands will help you to stay focused. Chanting a chant like om mani padme hum is usually done 108 times to help you enter trance.

Beads are also used while chanting. There are usually 108 beads on a chain. You count each bead every time you say the chant. Again, this helps you stay focused. By using your hands, altering your conscious raises your vibration, clears your conscious, and tune you to access higher knowledge.

SCRYING

Scrying is a great tool for developing you clairvoyance "clear seeing," especially extra-sensory perception. Scrying is also easy and fun. You can scry with a bowl of water. Using a black bowl works best if doing water scrying. Put about one inch of water into your black bowl and then stare into the bowl. Keep your attention only on scrying, just sit very still and stare. Images will start to appear once you start getting comfortable.

It also works best to scry in a dark room with two lit candles. Put one on each side of the bowl, if you have long hair, tie it back or wear a bandanna or something. Just don't let your hair get into the flame.

Another awesome way to scry is with a black mirror. The only problem here, is that black mirrors are expensive. I made one myself, because it was a lot cheaper. I went to the local store and bought a 8x10 picture frame and a can of flat black spray paint.

Take the glass out of the picture frame and paint one side of the glass with the black spray paint. Allow the glass to dry. After the glass is dry, place the glass back into the picture frame with the painted side of the glass facing the back of the frame, then abracadabra, you have yourself a black mirror for a fraction of the price and it works and looks just as good as the store bought ones.

Set your mirror about six feet away from you, sit in a comfortable chair with your hand in you lap and just sit there and relax. As you stare into the mirror, your eyes will begin to go out of focus. That's okay, that is what you want them to do. As you get relaxed and your eyes go out of focus, you will begin to get tunnel vision and feel like you are being pulled into your mirror.

This is when the fun starts, you will start seeing images of people, places, and objects. While scrying, don't try to edit or censor anything, just allow it to flow and see what happens. It is extraordinary.

THE PENDULUM

Dowsing with a pendulum is another great way to scan the chakra. Pendulum's have been used since ancient times. They are very accurate when using them with the proper knowledge. I use one that is made out of copper and it works great. You can also use a ring, such as a wedding band, or something special to you.

You then need to tie a string around the item you are using. The string needs to be at least one foot long. Use plain sheet of paper. Place the string in between your index finger and your thumb. Hold the pendulum about 6 inches above the paper.

Then ask the pendulum to show you yes, and it will swing in that direction. Make a note on the paper of the direction it swings and write yes. Then ask it to show you no and write that down as well.

If you haven't worn the ring for awhile, it may not be properly in tune with your vibration. You will need to wear the ring on a necklace so it will rest against your heart chakra. After a couple of days, try to dowse again, you will be amazed with the strong movement of it.

You can start asking the pendulum questions, after you have found out which way is yes and which way is no. You can tell the pendulum to stop before proceeding to the next question, and it will stop.

Using the pendulum for dowsing chakras: the crown chakra rotates clockwise, so if the pendulum swings counterclockwise, it may indicate that it is out of balance; the third eye also spins clockwise, throat chakra spins counterclockwise, heart chakra spins clockwise, the solar plexus chakra spins clockwise, the sacral chakra spins clockwise, and the base chakra spins counterclockwise.

If your pendulum swings in the opposite direction, it likely indicates that the chakra in question is most likely out of balance. If it swings too fast in the right direction, it could be an indication of an over stimulated chakra.

NUMEROLOGY

Numerology is a way of calculating your birth number. To do this, add the month, day, and year. For example: May 15th, 1965, you would add 5+1+5+1+9+6+5=32, and then add the total 32, 3+2=5. Five would be your birth number.

To calculate your growth number, add your birthday and the current year together. For example: May 15th, 2007, you would add 5+1+5+2+0+0+7=2.

In numerology the growth year goes up to 21, so any numbers after 21 on your growth year would be reduced by adding, say for example, your growth year added up to be 26, you would add 2+6=8, so your personal year would be 8.

There are a lot of very good sources out there for numerology meanings. You are able to find out a lot about yourself through the use of numbers and the vibrations they attract. It is very interesting and accurate to use numerology.

OVERCOMING EGO

This one is a biggie for a lot of people, because they don't realize it until they stick their foot in their mouth, so to speak. The ego is the part of you that thinks it is better or more deserving, better looking or better built, prettier or the know it all, or the authority figures on their power trip. Not all people in authority have issues with ego, "the big head."

Here is how I found out about my ego. When I was twenty-one years old, I was a kick boxer, nothing special. I was training, like a lot of the students, our trainer always told us to be humble. But, boy did I ever forget that one night.

I was training for a fight and my sparring partner Ed and I were having a great work out. We were in the fifth round, and I noticed my girlfriend at the time, who is now my wife, walked in to watch us spar. As she was watching, I wanted to show her that I was good and that I wanted to try and prove myself in the ring, so she would think I was a macho man.

I started picking up the pace, hitting and kicking with everything I had in me. Ed was older than me so he knew what was going on, not to mention, I would have never hit someone like that unless it was for a real match.

Well, Ed started moving faster, dodging my kicks and punches. I was hitting nothing but air and finally the mat. As Ed threw the last left hook of the night, the next thing I knew, Lisa, was leaned over top of me in the corner, asking me if I was okay.

After I got up, I went to the dressing room. Ed was in there changing, I felt so bad because Ed was my friend and I tried to make myself appear to be better than him. I thought that I may have lost his trust.

I went over to Ed and shook his hand and told him I knew I
deserved it. Ed said, "I know you did, because I did the same thing along time ago, to show off in front of this girl that I liked." We just laughed it off. He told me that next time, it was going to be just me and him training and no girlfriends were allowed.

Ego in meditation works pretty much the same way. With you sitting there trying to clear your mind and that little voice in you head says, I could be watching TV or anything but this. Or I don't know why I do this or thinking that no one else in my family meditates, they might think that I am crazy.

Any negative self talk like that is your ego. Your spirit wants to be there because you are. And your ego tries to get you to leave unless it is a real emergency. Just set it out, that negative self talk will go away. Then your mind will begin to clear and focused.

Your ego is like a little child running around when you have company, trying to show off. So, you handle it the same way, put it in time out. Say to yourself, this is my spirits time. My ego is in time out until I finish my meditation.

Don't learn about the ego the hard way like me. Remember the saying, if the right hand offends you, cut it off. Well, it is talking about your ego, if it offends you, put a stop to it.

Part III

True Stories

Chapter 9

Christy's Reading

When I first started doing my readings professional, my wife and I owned and operated our own tanning salon. One day while I was working, a young lady named Christy came in to get the prices on some tanning sessions. As she was starting to leave, she noticed one of my business cards for psychic readings on the counter. She reached down and picked one up and turned back and looked at me with a huge smile. She said she had been thinking a lot lately about getting a reading done. She also said she didn't know where to go or who to call to get a reading from.

Christy started asking me questions about how long had I been doing reading, and wanted to know how much it cost to get a reading done. I told her how much I charged and what all I did. She said she didn't have the money right now, but would get it and call and make an appointment with me.

Then my spirit guided jumped in and told me to do a reading for her, that she desperately needed one done. So, I asked her if she had time to talk for a little while, and she said yes. I asked her to have a seat and I would give her a reading and not charge her anything.

I then asked her if I could hold her ring, she handed me her ring and then sat down. I sat down, closed my eyes and took a few deep relaxing breaths. Then as I sat there, the words started to flow. I heard the voice of a little boy. I told her that there was a little boy here and he tells me to tell my sissy that I am here and that I am okay. I then heard the gentle little voice say to me, I was a baby when I passed away. I then told Christy what he had just told me. She then busted out into tears and said, he is my little brother and he passed away when he was just an infant.

The little boy then said, tell her I hear her when she talks to me and tells me she loves me and that she hopes that I am okay wherever I am
at. I began telling her, she told me she had cold chills really bad then. She told me that when she prays, I always say, if you can hear me, I love you and I
miss you very much.

She then asked me if he wanted to tell her anything else. The little angelic voice then replied, tell her daddy's going to be okay. I then told her what he just told me. Christy said that was good, she had been so worried about her dad lately.

She asked if he was still there, and I told her that he was. Christy asked me if he had told me his name, and I said no he hadn't, before I could finish telling Christy this, I heard the little voice tell me his name was Adam. I told her that he told me his name was Adam. She said, "oh my God". I told her he is still here with us and he hears me and he also hears everything that she says. Christy could not believe it, she said she was so amazed.

Her face lit up and I gave her the ring back. I told her that I hoped that I was able to help her. She said oh, yes, it was so amazing, now I feel much better. She said that she was so worried about her dad and missed her baby brother so much. She said now I know why I came in here, Adam sent
me to you. Christy then stretched out her arms and gave me a big tight hug, and said, now I know that prayers really do get answered. She had the biggest smile on her face as she left.

After Christy left, I started thinking, "wow", that little spirit brought her right in here, because she needed to hear that really bad. I was not worried about the pay or anything like that, it was just my vibes that told me to just do it and I did. Just knowing that I was able to help her find the answers she was looking for was an awesome feeling to me. This turned out to be a beautiful outcome.

Chapter 10

SARA'S READING

One evening last fall, I had an appointment with this young lady named Sara. When Sara arrived, she seemed pretty calm and relaxed. She was even joking around, as we sat down to do the Tarot reading. I told Sara to just think of what she wanted the reading to be focused on. She then shuffled the cards, for what seemed like forever.

I then started reading the cards. They indicated that communication was the major issue at hand and that there was a communication block. The cards also indicated a choice to be made between two issues and about a man with brown hair and blue eyes.

As I started explaining the meaning of the cards, Sara begin to look at me like, this is for real. Sara gave me her total attention during the reading. The card, returning to a communication block came up at least three times in the reading.

After the reading was over, I asked Sara if it had answered her question. She said, "well", with a really surprised look, then said, "I asked if I was going to have anymore children." "But you know, the whole time I was shuffling the cards, I couldn't stay focused on my question." "Because there is this guy I met at work and we have sort of been seeing each other, and I didn't know how to tell my husband about it." "I wanted to tell him, not to get me wrong, but I was really scared about how he is going to take it, because I am planning on moving out and filing for a divorce."

Just then, Sara's cell phone rang, it was her husband calling her and he wanted to know where she was at, because she was suppose to be at work. She had called in to work sick, so she could get her and her
baby's belongings out of her house. After she ended the conversation
with her husband, she said, "I am about to freak out." She then begin to tell me, she did everything she normally did when she leaves for work, so her husband would not suspect her of anything.

Sara's husband told her that his vibes told him that there was something wrong, so he thought he would call her and check on her. He also asked , if she would talk with him, that they never communicate with each other anymore.

Sara then said to me, "well I better go home now, it looks like I have some communicating to do.

Chapter 11

"HOLY SMOKE BATMAN"

In February of last year, a woman in her late thirty's came to me for a reading. As this lady sit down, I felt a very depressing energy as I began the reading, I kept hearing the name
Charlie and car accident. I then told her, that I kept hearing the name "Charlie and that he was telling me, car accident."

She looked at me like she was in shock, she then started crying. I asked her if she was okay. She said yes, fighting back the tears, she began to tell me that her husbands name was Charlie and that he died in a car accident.

Charlie was telling me "three girls." The lady said, "yes, we had three daughters together." Then the reading went cold, but I thought I kept on hearing, batman, batman. Since I went cold, I got my tarot cards out and did the Celtic cross spread.

As we were discussing the reading, I still kept hearing the words batman. I just ignored it and kept on doing the tarot reading. I then finished the tarot reading and the lady was getting ready to leave, she asked me if anything weird or strange ever happens to me when I am doing a reading.

I said, "yes, as a matter of fact, during your reading, I kept hearing the words batman." She put her hand over her mouth, and took a huge gasp or air. She told me, that when her husband Charlie was young, his family had been really poor and when they got married, the only thing he had left from his childhood, was a complete set of batman cards, that his grandfather had bought for him.

She then went on to say, "just last night, my oldest daughter, whose name is Charley, and I were up late talking about her father, and that she had gotten her dad's cards out. Because when she holds them she feels her dad's energy, and it felt like he was right there in the room with her."

As she left, she thanked me for the reading, and that she said she feels so much better knowing that he is still here watching over her and her girls.

Chapter 12

BECKY'S READING

Last summer I had an appointment to do a reading for this lady named Becky. When Becky walked in, she looked very sad. As I started doing the reading, the first thing that I heard was, "tell her dad's here." I told her what I heard and she said that was why she came to me, because, her dad had passed away.

I started seeing power lines and a boat. I asked Becky if her dad was an Electrician. She said, "yes, I cant believe this." I noticed a smile come on her face, then her eyes started sparkling. She didn't look the same as she did when she first walked in.

I continued with her reading. Her dad then tells me, to tell his daughter, that he liked the keepsake box that she had made. I told her what her dad was saying, she very excitedly said, "oh my, I just finished it, I made it to put his jewelry in. I wanted to make a keepsake box for my dad's things.

He also went on to tell me, to tell pancake to cheer up and to stop grieving over him, and to spend time with his grandkids.

I told her that, and she said that she couldn't help it, she said she loves him so much. She also told me that she hasn't spent much time with her girls lately.

She asked me to tell him that she would start spending more time with the girls and that she loved and missed him very much.

I told her that I didn't have to tell him, she just did, that he hears everything she says. She was so happy and she started to smile.

Becky said that she had been watching TV shows about psychics and wanted to see for herself if it was for real or not.

She thanked me for her reading, and told me that everything I told her was true, and that no-one could ever convince her otherwise.

Chapter 13

DREAMS

Most of our dreams are very psychic in nature. The best way to prove this to yourself is to take notes on your dreams. You might want to keep a journal in your bedroom to record your dreams in it. You will want to write down your dreams as soon as you get up before you forget them. Unless they are really vivid, you will probably forget them as the days go on.

There are a lot of dream interpretation books out there. However, they may not be too accurate for you. So, if you keep your dream journal updated you will start to notice patterns in your dreams and the meaning of them, as well.

People may come to you in your dreams and offer you very intuitive guidance. It is important to remember that all dreams are not intuitive in nature. They could have been caused by a stressful day at work or at home.

You will notice these dream patterns as well. In other words, just because you have a bad dream, does not mean it is going to happen at all. It just simply means you have been under too much stress and you need to correct the situation that is causing you to have dreams of a negative nature.

THE DREAM ABOUT MY BROTHER

It was the summer of 2001. I woke up having a very bad dream about my brother Tim. I was dreaming that he was laying in a ditch with blood on his forehead and a cut above his left eye. I also seen him reaching his left hand out toward me saying, "help me Michael."
The dream bothered me a lot.

I had to work that day, so I got ready and left. When I got to work, I told my co-worker, who was also my friend, about my dream. I was telling him how vivid and disturbing it was.

About five minutes had passed and I got a phone call from Tim. I was surprised to hear his voice on the phone, since I hadn't talked to him for at least a couple of months. We talked for a few minutes and he asked me if he could borrow my truck so the could move some furniture. I told him that he could. About an hour later he came and picked up my truck and left.

About six hours later he returned my truck to me at my house and he thanked me for letting him use my truck. He hung out for a few minutes and we talked, and then he left to go home.

It was three o'clock in the morning, I got woke up by the phone. It was my oldest sister, Tammy. She had called to tell me that Tim had been in a car accident and that they had to fly him to Louisville, Kentucky, and that he was in critical condition.

I woke Lisa up, and we went to pick up my youngest sister, Jackie, and we drove to Louisville to be with Tim.

As we arrived at the hospital, we could see Tim in the emergency room. He was laying on a gurney unconscious. He had a cut above his left eye and there was blood on his forehead. Just like in my dream I had the night before. My sister, Tammy came into the waiting room and told us what all happened. She then told me that the police officer that worked the accident said that Tim had his hand reached out to him, asking for Michael. The officer asked Tim who Michael was.

Tim told him it was his little brother, and that he worked at the County Jail. The officer couldn't get anything else from him, because he was going in and out of consciousness.

We spent a few hours at the hospital to make sure Tim was going to be okay. After a few weeks in the hospital, Tim got to go home.

Thank God, Tim recovered from the wreck and he is doing fine now.

Chapter 14

Healing

A few months ago, this girl named Beverly, came to my tanning salon, and she was holding her left hand, with her right hand. She was in tears and asked me if there was something I could do to ease her pain.

She told me that she had been to her family doctor two days prior and he x-rayed her hand and he told her that it was fractured. He also told her that they couldn't put a cast on it until the swelling went down.

Beverly then said that her doctor gave her some pain medication, but it wasn't helping the pain any at all.

I asked Beverly if I could see her hand, so she took the bandage wrap off and reached her hand out to me. The whole time, she was crying huge tears, because of the pain.

I asked Beverly to hold her hand out and that I would try something. She asked me if it would hurt, and I told her that it wouldn't, that I wasn't even going to touch it.

I gently rubbed my hands together and said an invocation prayer. I moved the palms of my hands over her hand.

She stopped crying and she started to move her hand, first her fingers and then her wrist. She looked straight at me, eyes wide open, and said that it wasn't hurting her anymore. Beverly said, "oh my God, it doesn't hurt at all!" She than began to laugh. She said, "that's crazy, how on earth did you do that?"

I told her it was by the grace of God, and energy. Beverly said, "those stupid pills didn't help not one bit, but you sure took away my pain. Thank you so much!"

She stayed awhile and we talked about everything. Then she had to leave and she left without a tear in sight.

Healing Energy

There are several different healing techniques that work very well in healing and re-balancing the aura and chakra.

Hands on healing, briskly rub the palms of your hands together for about thirty seconds and then shake them like you are shaking water off of them. Then briskly rub your palms together again for another thirty seconds. Place your hands, palms down, about one inch above the person you are directing your energy towards. Be sure to keep your mind on clearing and rebalancing the energy in the specific area you are working on. Remembering to go in the proper direction of the chakra focused on. You may wish to do this a couple of times on each chakra.

The next technique is the use of healing stones and crystals. Use the same color of stone that represents each chakra and clear crystals. Place them on each chakra point of the body.

Both of these techniques work very well and they both have phenomenal healing vibration. They also help you set your intention and attention on the healing process, and where your attentions goes, your energy will follow.

Have the person needing the energy healing lay flat on his or her back, and then place the crystals or colored stones on each of the chakra's that need healed, or you can place them on all of the chakra's.

I always have the person being healed to place the stones or crystals on their own chakra's, this way they are more comfortable. After doing the front of the person, have them lay on their stomach, and do the same with the chakra's on the backside. They are all located over the back the same way they are on the front.

You may also want to turn on some music that is healing, and light some candles that have the same color vibration of the chakra's being healed. I found that Indian drum and flute music work very well for this. You may also wish to use scented oils. Have the person to smell the oils you have and let them find the one that is most relaxing for them.

I truly believe most people need energy healing. Living in today's fast paced life style is wearing us all down., with work, kids, cooking, cleaning, grocery shopping and every day things.

Our generation thinks they have always got to be doing something, such as, playing on the computer, talking on their cell phone and run, run, run. We all get caught up in this drama and forget that we are the very ones that caused all of the rushing around in the first place.

Some of the most effective healing for body, mind and spirit is rest. This is why people go to a energy healer, because they want to sit down and relax. Most people cannot do this at home, with the TV blaring, demands of husbands and wives, our kids school, karate, baseball, football, basketball, and dances.

There is no time for yourself. So, people go to healers to be healed and they are healed. It all starts with their attention and thoughts of wanting to be healed and like I said before, where your attention goes, your energy follows. Even if your energy is low and you need healing. Your energy will the pull the stronger healing energy toward you, and you will find your healing energy source. That's the law of the universe.

WILLIAMS ARM

Last fall this man named William came in to tan, at my tanning salon. He was a regular customer that came in often to tan.

William showed me this huge knot that was just below his left elbow. It was big and it literally looked like it was the size of a golf ball under his skin. He had his arm drawn up to his side.

William works on a horse farm and he told me that a huge stud jumped up and kicked him full force. He said it happened about 9:30 a.m., and here it was 8:00 p.m., when he came into the tanning salon.

William and I have been friends for awhile, but he had never asked me for a healing, I just did readings for him.

On this day, he must have really been in pain because he asked me if I would try to heal his arm with healing energy. I told him, of course. So, I said an invocation prayer and rubbed my hands together slightly, and held them about a half inch above the knot. I maybe done this for a least one minute.

I stopped, and shook my hands out. Then, William started moving his arm and said there was no pain at all, and that he couldn't believe it.

William said, "it has hurt me all day long and you do that and it just stops, wow!" We just stood there and laughed about that horse kicking him.

As William walked to the door to get into the tanning bed,

he kept moving his arm and was looking at me suspiciously and then he just started laughing again.

He tanned for 10 minutes, and to both of our surprise, that knot was completely gone. Now that was really awesome.

I thank the divine mother, the divine father and my healer guides for allowing me to source from them to heal not just my friends, but everyone that has come to me in need of healing.

HEALING JACKIE'S BACK

My younger sister Jackie came to visit me and my family one night. We sat around and talked for awhile. She then told me that her back had been hurting her ever since she got up that morning.

Jackie doesn't complain, so I knew that it had to be hurting her pretty bad for her to even say anything about it. I then asked her where on her back did it hurt, and she told me it was her lower back on the right side. She said that she thought she pulled a muscle.

I asked her if she wanted me to try my energy healing on her back, and she told me that I could try. I had her lay flat on her stomach, and I began saying a invocation prayer, and used energy healing.

Jackie told me, that as soon as I placed my hands over her back, she could feel her muscles stretch out like rubber bands. She also told me that it felt really strange.

As she was talking to me about it, she said that it was weird, she said, "Michael, look," she was reaching out her arm for me to look, she had cold chills, she said that she never got cold chills before.

Jackie said, "oh my God, that is so unreal, as soon as the cold chills went away, my pain went away." She was so amazed that I could even do energy healing. It is a wonderful feeling, knowing I could help make her feel better.

Later that night when Jackie went to leave, she told me that her back felt so much better, and that now she could get some sleep.

PRAYING FOR RICK

My friend Rick asked me to come over to his house and do my energy healing and pray for his eyes. He can't see very well. He told me that his doctor had told him that he was going blind. Of course this just devastated Rick.

I went over to his house for prayer and to do my energy healing for him. I had him lay down on his couch, and I placed a clear quartz crystal on his forehead. I had written a special prayer for him, so I began praying for him, and I used energy healing on his third eye chakra.

You could instantly feel the vibration start to rise in the room. As I finished the prayer and healing, Rick opened his eyes very quickly. His eyesight was still the same. Both of us were expecting a miracle to take place instantly.

It didn't quite happen the way that we were hoping that it would. When Rick raised up his head, he said, "I have got to tell you something. When you were praying for me I mentally saw a huge polar bear standing over me, it was the neatest thing that I have ever seen before. I have never before seen images like that."

Several months has passed since that night. Since then, Rick has written several country songs, and even has some very famous people wanting to buy his lyrics.

Rick told me, since that day of the healing energy and prayer, he see's visions in his mind and they inspire him to write music. Rick also told me that his doctor has told him there is a new procedure out and he is pretty sure it will help Rick regain his eyesight.

I wish the very best for Rick, and may God bless him and be with him.

Chapter 15

ANTIQUE CLOCK

When my grandmother, Nanny passed away, I was given a mantel clock that belonged to her. It was very beautiful and very old clock. It was built in 1814. I could not stow it away in a box like my nanny had done.

I placed it on my dresser in my bedroom. The really cool thing about it was the chime. It was a very deep chime and it sounded just like church bells. It still works well and everything, but I didn't keep it wound. I just had it sitting out for looks.

One night, I was relaxing in a warm bath with lavender and Epsom salt. It was very quite in the house that night. When out of the blue, I felt my grandmother presence, which was very comfortable to me.

I thought to myself, I miss her so much, then I started thinking about something else, so I wouldn't get all emotional. When the antique clock started chiming, it chimed twelve times. The really neat thing was it was twelve o'clock on my wall clock in the bathroom. But my grandmothers clock, the one that chimed, was not running, it wasn't even wound and the hands were stopped at twelve o'clock.

It was really assuring I have to say. But at first, I must have looked like a scared cat with my hair standing up. I believe that's the way my nanny would have wanted it, she always did like to sneak up on people when she was living. Just the thought of scaring someone, she thought it was funny.

I ended up giving my sister Billie the clock, because her and my grandmother were very close.

CALLING ON ANGELS

One week while I was studying the alien and UFO phenomenon, I began getting stressed. I figured that it was mostly due to the fact that I love to learn and when I get interested in a subject, I will dig and dig to get more information.

Even though I have had a couple of experiences with the phenomenon myself. I wanted to learn about other peoples experiences.

Being a psychic myself, I have been taught to stay grounded and not to live in my head alone over analyzing things.

This week, I slipped up and became over analytical and was not getting enough exercise. I wasn't grounded and when that happens it is not good at all. You will start getting aggravated and anxious and will even start having anxiety.

I then stopped what I was doing, went outside and walked at a fast pace for maybe a half hour, and then I went back inside, turned up the stereo on the 80's channel and started cleaning and organizing things, that I had neglected to do.

During that week, the more I worked, the more grounded I had become. I heard the voice of my higher self telling me not to forget to call on my angels for help as well.

So, I get a book on archangels out and did the usual. I said a prayer asking the divine mother and the divine father to guide me to the angel or archangel that would best help with that situation.

I did not look down at the book, I just started flipping

pages until my higher self told me to stop. I then looked down and found archangel Sandalphon. If you are not familiar with Sandalphon, it may be because of the name change. His name in the bible is Elijah. Elijah was ascended into heaven in a fiery chariot.

There is a reference to this in 2 kings in the King James version. There appeared a chariot of fire and horses of fire. Elijah went up by a whirlwind into heaven.

Now if this doesn't sound strange, how about this, "Sandalphon Elijah" also helps with deliverance, which in my case, was the over analyzing and anxiety from not being grounded.

So, if you want to learn, by all means, do so but remember to back off at times and give your mind a break and get back into your body. This will keep you balanced. Like the saying, man can't live off of bread alone. Bread meaning knowledge, get out and be psychical as well and don't neglect your body.

Chapter 16

NEGATIVE ENERGY

This lady named Trinity came to me for a reading. Her husband of 4 years had left her. She was very depressed and upset. She told me she didn't know what happened, one day he just up and left. During the reading, which was indicating a lot of negative mental energy the card death rebirth came up. This is not a bad card, though. I continued the reading for her.

Trinity told me that the energy around her home feels so thick and very negative. And that she thought that it was just her over analyzing everything.

After the reading was over, I told her about using smudge sticks and how she could bless her home. She wanted to know if I was sure that it would work. I told her that it does work very well. I gave her a bundle of the white sage, so she could smudge her home.

I told her to smudge her house and to just relax and know that this would work. After I explained everything to her on how to do the smudging, I left.

Three days later after Trinity's reading, I saw her. Her husband was with her. That's right, they got back together. She whispered to me if she could speak to me for a minute.

She stepped a little closer and smiled at me. She begin to tell me about her smudging her house, and that no sooner than she put out the smudge stick and sat down to relax, she heard a knock at the door. She opened it and to her surprise it was her husband.

She said that they sat and talked for hours until it was daylight. Trinity also told me that she never told her husband anything bout the smudge stick and ironically enough, Ted, my husband, said that he didn't know if it was just him or what, but the energy around them felt so negative. And that he just couldn't take it. Then he told her that it felt a lot different now.

As far as the death rebirth card, they ended up getting back together and that they are going to renew their wedding vows soon.

So, if the energy in your home feels heavy, thick or stuck, try smudging your house, it works very well.

CLEARING NEGATIVE ENERGY

There are many different ways to clear negative energy. First you need to identify the source. If you are able to identify the source and you are able to leave the source, then you need to leave. If leaving would not be practical, you could burn some white sage and allow the smoke to fill the air in the area. This is called smudging. You should even smudge yourself.

You can buy sage in a bundle or loosely. If you buy the bundle, light the bundle at one end, like an incense. Then allow the sage to burn for a few seconds and then blow it out. It will then begin to smoke, while it is smoking, walk through your house with it. You may want to hold a plate or something under it to catch any falling ashes. Make sure you get all the corners as well.

You may also want to light a white candle and allow it to burn until it burns out on its own. Take the remaining wax that is left after the candle has burnt all the way out by itself and take it off of your property and dispose of it. Because it catches all the negative energy. Remember to never leave your candle unattended.

You can also use regular household salt, by pouring it around your property line. You do not need to use very much of the salt, just make a small trail with it.

My teacher, Sonia, told me to use Epsom salt and lavender in my bath. You use about 1 cup of Epsom salt and a couple drops of lavender oil. Then soak in the tub for about twenty minutes. The Epsom salt absorbs the negative energy and it balances your aura. The lavender helps you relax. As you are soaking in the tub, picture the negative energy being pulled from you body into the salt crystals.

EXERCISE

Exercise burns away negative thought patterns. If you are consistently thinking or worrying or even obsessing, chances are you are living in you head alone and you are not spending enough time in you body.

You should exercise for at least 30 minutes per day. This will dramatically lower your stress levels and release the toxins in you body through your sweat glands.

The shamans believe your sweat glands are your bodies third kidney. I find this to be true as well, so get out there and swim, jog, run, do something that makes you sweat and gets your heart beating at you target heart rate. You could ask you doctor or personal trainer, they could tell you what you ideal heart rate should be and how long to keep it at that rate.

It will reduce body fat and keep your stress levels down to a minimum. This will really sharpen your intuitive channels. We all function greater when our stress levels are down. It also helps focus your attention for meditation.

BANISHING NEGATIVE ENERGY

We all have had that special someone, that just won't leave us alone and continues to cause trouble in our lives. And you say you want to stop them from sending negative energy your way or from even coming around you.

My grandmother, Nanny, taught me this magic, that seems to work for me. First, you could write down something like this, I, (your name), set my attention and intention on burning out the negative energy coming from, (person's name).

After you have written it down, place it in a kitchen sink, if it is metal, if not, use an old pan or something that is metal. Then light the paper and watch it burn until it turns to all ashes. Then, wash the ashes down the drain, allowing the water to run for a couple of minutes, to flush it out of you pipes and off of your property.

If possible, putting the ashes in a river or creek and allow the ashes to flow away from you. This is a very powerful tool against negative energy and it does work very well.

You can also rid negative energy projected towards you by writing it down, as I mentioned earlier and put it in a jar of water and add some blue food coloring and freeze it. You should leave it frozen until you feel comfortable taking it out. Doing this helps set your intention and attention on your desired outcome.

Just remember, where your attention goes your energy follows. The water and food coloring are just tools to help you set your attention. Some people can accomplish this just by thinking about it. But, myself, I prefer to use tools to help get my attention and set my intention and it has always worked for me.

I was fortunate enough to have a grandmother that taught me this at a young age. Knowledge is power.

You could also use kind of the same principal to help set your attention on a particular goal. Before I started writing this book, I got some construction paper and cut out a rectangle and made it to look like the cover of a book and I put it on my bedroom wall, so that every time I was in my bedroom, I would see it and think about writing my book. It gets my attention and reminds me of my intentions. I hope you see what I mean.

RAISING YOUR VIBRATION

When I feel my vibration needs maintenance, I start cleaning out everything and start getting rid of stuff I no longer need. I bring flowers in , clean the house, do the yard work, organize things, and play some classical music.

I also like to have my beautiful wife and my 3 wonderful boys sit down with me and we each name off ten things that our spirit loves. Just listening to my wife and my boys tell me what their spirits love, instantly opens my heart chakra.

They tell me it does theirs as well. We will also sit at the kitchen table and have supper together. We even bless our food together. While eating we always turn off the television and the phone so we won't be bothered.

My wife and I also like to take a relaxing bath with candles lit. We all also like to sit at the kitchen table with a coloring book and just hang out and color with our boys. Doing these things when energy feels stuck., will bring balance back into your life, and will make the energy start flowing again with good vibrations. So, try this and allow the higher energies that are knocking to come in.

Chapter 17

SEEING AND READING THE AURA

Your aura is electro magnetic. You want to have your subject stand about two feet away from a plain white wall. It is best to use a 60 watt light standard light bulb. For the best results, you should stand at least 8 to 10 feet away from your subject. Then you allow your eyes to go out of focus, like when you look at a 3D picture.

Look about 2 inches above the subjects head. Within a few minutes, you should be able to see the aura. If it is hard to see, you may have the subject to move from side to side in a swaying motion. Usually it comes into view. Once you get use to that, then you will be able to see the aura and colors easier. You can also look about 2 inches around the subjects body and see the aura.

If you want to feel the aura, first you need to gently rub your hands together, then shake them out and rub them together again. Move your hands, palms facing the subject, about two inches away from the person, you should be able to feel their energy.

*Colors and meanings of the aura

Red - anger, hostility, anxiety, lust, nervousness, relates to physical body, when working properly will be able to think quickly in survival situations.

Orange - sexual and reproductive organs, vigor energy.

Yellow - psychic intuitive, awakening, artistic, fun, laughter will also power.

Green - healing energy, heart and repertory system.
Bright green - also love emotions and the seat of the soul.

Blue - (neck and throat) clear speaking, singing, also related to intelligence, innovative wisdom, visionary, intuitive.

Indigo - (third eye) intuitive dreams, including, daydreams and fantasy ability to look deep inside yourself and others.

Purple or Violet - (top of head or crown) intuitive psychic ability, wisdom, high spiritual color.

SCANNING YOUR BODYS ENERGY
FIELDS "CHAKRA'S

Dowsing rods are very helpful and was used by the ancients to find water and to retrieve lost animals. Dowsing was used in Vietnam to locate missing soldiers. They are currently used today, even though there are digital scanning devices. Some people say that they are more dependable than any modern devices out there.

To make your own dowsing rods, go to you local hardware store and buy, 2- two foot long copper rods, about the same diameter as a wire cloths hanger. Bend one end on both of the rods about 6 inches up. They should look like an "L" shape. Then you slide the end that is not bent down the middle of a small tube. I found that removing the ink tube and ends out of an ink pen and using the ink pen tube works great. You will need to cut the ink pen tub to 5 inches long. Using a pair of pliers bend the small ends that are sticking out of the pen tube in the shape of another "L". This will keep the rod from slipping out of the tube.

Once you have done this, you are ready to start experimenting with your dowsing rods. You will need to hold the ink pen tube one in each hand, straight out in front of you, with your arms straight, and elbows locked. Your thumbs should be pointing up and wrapped around the handle of you dowsing rods. Now you are ready to practice.

Have someone stand about 10 feet away from you. Hold the dowsing rods up, shoulder height and width apart, and try to hold your hands steady. Have that person to start walking toward you. You will be able to notice when their aura fields connect with the rods. Your dowsing rods will start swinging either clockwise or counterclockwise.

As the person gets closer, the rods should cross in the middle.

Experiment with them until you become familiar with it. Then you will be able to scan different chakra's, to see how strong each chakra energy field is. Be careful not to accidentally poke someone or yourself with the long ends of the rods. Some people bend the long ends about half an inch from the end so they don't poke someone with them.

Make sure, that the person you are scanning does not have any jewelry on, because this could throw it off some, especially if they are wearing crystals. Have the person stand about 6 feet away from you and allow them to take small steps towards you. Pointing the dowsing rods towards the chakra's you want to measure. The chakra's that are functioning properly will swing the rods apart at a steady pace.

Under active chakra's, the rods will move very slow and bounce. Over active chakra's, they will swing too fast. You will be able to notice the difference once you have done this a few times. You may also practice on a bowl of water, plants, trees, and even pets, to measure the chakra's. While dowsing, be sure to always keep your mind on what you are doing and stay focused.

I am sure the dowsing rods will work like a charm every time. Try this, it is extraordinary and very fun as well.

SEVEN MAJOR CHAKRAS/MUSICAL NOTES

Crown - B

Third eye - A

Throat - G

Heart - F

Solar Plexus - E

Sacral - D

Root - C

MUSICAL NOTE FREQUENCY

Crown - 494 HZ

Third eye - 440 HZ

Throat - 392 HZ

Heart - 349 HZ

Solar Plexus - 330 HZ

Root - 262 HZ

CHAKRA LOCATIONS AND COLORS

The chakra system, there is seven chakras that go down the middle of your body

The crown chakra is bright white.

The root chakra, lower animal energy also is in the location where kundalini begins to rise. Starting at the base of your spine. This chakra is red, which is like fire, it is your survival energy chakra. Out of balance could cause restlessness, anger, anxiety, and lack of patience. The letter E sounds like "eh" like when you are relaxing after a long day and you sit down and sigh.

Sacral chakra, is located at about 3 inches below your navel. This chakra is orange. Fertility, sex, reproducing our primitive animal needs. Sounds like "O" as in Rome.

Solar plexus or wheel chakra, self confidence, laughter, just remember it is your wheel for this to be done. Mantra is ram/aum. The color of this chakra is bright yellow.

Heart chakra, sound ahh, like when you see a beautiful baby for the first time. The color of this chakra is green, "emerald."

The throat chakra is located at the base of your throat. This chakra is sky blue.

Brow chakra, third eye, the color is indigo, like midnight on a full moon.

Crown chakra, is like a rainbow that changes colors of the six other colors of the chakra system, bright.

SOUNDS OF CHAKRAS

Om - upward and outward

Krim "kreem" - lower chakra's

Shrim "shreem" - third eye

Hrim "herem" - purify the heart

Hum "hoom" - destroys negativity

Root chakra - lam
Sacral chakra - van, hands up on lap
Navel chakra -Ram, hands together pointing out

Heart chakra - sit cross legged tops of index and thumbs touch left hand on left knee, right hand lower part of breast bone chant, "yam"

Throat chakra - cross fingers on the inside of your hands, pull thumbs up and chant, "ham"

Third eye - "om" or "aum", thumbs together, index bent and together, middle fingers up

Open crown - hands before stomach, let ring fingers point up touching at tops, cross the rest of your fingers, left thumb under right thumb, and chant "ng" sounds like "ning"

Open root chakra - before opening crown chakra, for best results do them in order starting at the root chakra.

TAROT READINGS

When doing a tarot reading, I use the Celtic cross spread. It is what most card readers use.

The first card represents the person being read.

The second card represents the direction the energy is moving, either negative or positive.

The third card represents the past.

The fourth card represents the present.

The fifth card represents what crowns this person, and what may come to pass.

The sixth card represents what will come to pass.

The seventh card represents what the person hopes for.

The eight card represents what the person fears.

The ninth card represents the families opinion, and the way the family see's the situation.

The tenth card represents the final outcome. Remember, the final outcome may change anything in motion, and you can change if you want too.

There are 22 major arcane cards, counting the fool card which is number 0.

There are four suits:
*Cups - emotional
*Wands - spiritual
*Pentacle or Disk - physical
*Swords - mental

There are several great books on tarot readings. This just touches the basics, I recommend you shop around and buy a deck and a book that you feel drawn to.

To Lisa
Love

Your spirit is beautiful like the humming bird,
Free and gentle, it says I love you, yet it doesn't speak a word.
Ever searching for something sweet,
The love you give is my hearts treat.
Your love is like the sea, deep and full of life,
Together we'll swim to find the key to life.
Lisa, it is you I hold dear,
Your angelic voice is the sound angels make when they
appear.
Our three son's we waited so long to see,
Yet they look at us and it is our own eyes we see.
They love you with all of their soul,
You say I love you, they smile and say mommy I know,
With you and our boys, our love will forever grow.
Lisa, without your spirit love I would have never known,
I am sure with our three seeds love will be continually grown,
I thank God for your spirit, for it is the gift of love, to me
you have shown.

Love Always,
Michael

About the Author

Michael Dean *is psychic medium, teacher, and healer. He began experiencing the psychic phenomenon at the age of 6. In his early years, he learned from his grandmother, who was a natural psychic. He has studied under world-renowned psychic Sonia Choquette. He resides with his wife and three sons in Indiana.*

Contact information: email: **revdean17@yahoo.com**